Math Medley

Activities For Teaching
Beginning Math Skills & Concepts

by Sylvia Gay and Janet Hoelker

Incentive Publications, Inc.
Nashville, Tennessee

Cover by Becky Rüegger
Illustrations by Susan Eaddy

Library of Congress Catalog Card Number: 92-71470
ISBN 0-86530-216-2

CONTENTS

Preface

Mathematics, in the early years, should be an integral part of the child's daily school experiences. Just as language can be taught throughout the school day, mathematics can be an all-day affair. It can be integrated into areas such as art, fine and gross motor activities, language, cognition, socialization, and music.

Manipulation of objects by the child is mandatory when new mathematical concepts are introduced. The continued manipulation of materials is also highly recommended to reinforce established concepts.

"Hands-on" activities that are interesting and fun for the child will naturally facilitate comprehension. This book contains activities designed to increase children's comprehension of mathematical concepts while maintaining their interest levels.

Instructional Objectives:

1. To provide experiential activities designed to foster the development of mathematical concepts.

2. To allow children to discover mathematical principles.

3. To increase children's interest in mathematical concepts.

4. To help children discover the practical application of mathematical concepts.

Grade Levels:

Early Childhood, Special Education, Kindergarten, Preschool, Early Primary, At-Risk

1 Craft Stick

Each child picks a friend. One child lies on the floor with his/her arms extended above his/her head or at his/her side. The other child lays craft sticks end-to-end to see how many craft sticks it takes to "measure" the friend. Measure other items.

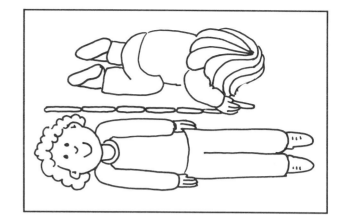

2 Big Mitten, Little Mitten

Have each child cut out a big paper mitten and a small paper mitten without using patterns. Attach mittens to hands with paper bands. The children should compare mittens with one another, noting which mittens are bigger and which ones are smaller.

3 Insect Count

Give each child two lettuce leaves, raisins for ants, and Chinese noodles for worms. Each child puts as many ants as he/she wishes on one leaf, and as many worms as desired on the other leaf. Compare and contrast with the other children's leaves.

4 Snack Count

Provide a variety of small snack items (sunflower seeds, tiny crackers, popcorn, etc.) for each child. Have the children count the items as they are passed out. Emphasize ordinal position by letting the children decide which they will eat first, second, last, etc.

Check-in
Have each child "check in" daily by putting a sticker under his/her name. Count the days present and absent.

JOE S.	JAN K.	DREW BY P.
☆		☆
	☆	☆

Long Legs
Ask the children to wear long-sleeved shirts and long pants to school. Have each child roll up one sleeve and one pantleg along with you. Then discuss *right, left, longer*, and *shorter.*

Cookie Eater
Cut out paper cookies (chocolate, vanilla, chocolate chip, etc.). Encourage each child to pick whichever cookie he/she wants and to "feed" it to a cookie eater of his/her design. Compare the numbers of different kinds of cookies that the cookie eater eats.

Flower Stems
Provide crepe paper for each child to make a flower stem as tall as he/she is. Let each child add a flower to the top of the stem. Tape the bottom of the stem to the inside of a "flowerpot" (a decorated paper cup, a plastic container, plastic planter, etc.) and the top to the wall. The flower should be equal to the child's height. Note which flowers are taller, shorter, the same height, etc.

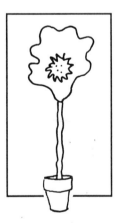

Shape People
Cut out various shapes from construction paper. Have the children divide themselves into groups of three or four. Give each group a variety of shapes, approximately five or ten of each. Have them ask each other for different shapes, which they should tape to their own bodies. Compare the "shape people."

10 Pattern Cup

Tape ten to twenty paper cups in a row on the floor or on a table. Have the children fill up alternate cups with sand, rice, birdseed, or styrofoam pieces. If necessary, color-code the cups white, red, white, red, etc. Have the children "read" the row: (Empty, full, empty, full, etc.)

11 Shoelace Skirts

Each child will need a belt. Have the children work in groups of three with a bag of shoelaces – short, medium, and long. Each child asks another for a specific length, which he/she then tapes or ties onto his/her belt. After the skirts have been made, compare the number of short, medium, and long shoelaces that each child has. (String or old ties may be used in place of shoelaces.)

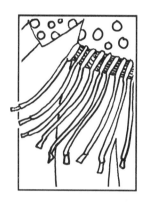

12 Feel The Numbers

Cut numerals out of foam rubber, wood, cardboard, or sandpaper. Have one child put a numeral inside a feely-box while the other children are not looking. A second child feels the numeral and claps, jumps, etc., a corresponding number of times. The other children silently count the actions and call out or write on sheets of paper how many they counted. A child takes the hidden numeral out for comparison.

13 I Feel

One child sits facing numerals appropriate for his/her level. A second child, standing behind him/her, pats him/her on the shoulder, back, arm, or head a certain number of times. The child who is sitting picks up the corresponding numeral.

Car Wash

Allow the children to make a car wash by cutting out the ends of a quart or half-gallon-sized milk carton and replacing them with string. You will need three to ten small cars which can fit through the car wash. Children may wish to work in groups of two. One child tells his/her partner how he/she should line up the cars before he/she can send them through the car wash. For example: Put the red car through first, the green car second, and last the yellow car. Ordinal positions should be emphasized.

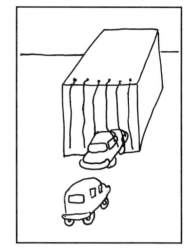

Grocery Bags

Collect food containers — canned food, boxes, bags, etc. You will need two of each kind, one empty and one full. Give the children two large grocery bags and ask them to put the full containers in one bag and the empty containers in the other bag.

Rhythm Sticks

Teach the children to hit rhythm sticks in time. Have them guess how many hits it will take for a child to complete a specific activity such as running around the room, skipping to the bathroom, drinking a glass of water, etc. Then hit the sticks together as the action is actually being completed. The children may clap, stamp their feet, or hit their desks instead of using rhythm sticks.

As Long As

Estimate how many cube blocks, toothpicks, pennies, styrofoam pieces, etc., it will take to measure the length of an object. Then measure to see how close the estimates are.

Fishbowls

Give a small group of children three plastic fishbowls. Provide a "fishing pond" (child's swimming pool or a piece of large paper cut in the shape of a pond). Put three different water creatures (such as fish, starfish, seahorses) into the pond. Have the children "go fishing" and sort their catches into the fishbowls.

19 Weigh-in

Purchase a scale or make a scale by punching three equally-spaced holes into each of two margarine tubs, attaching a string to each hole, and tying each three-string set to the corner of a hanger. Hang the hanger over a stick. Provide the children with heavy and light items, and let them freely manipulate and explore.

20 Pockets

Supply numerous rulers and large spoons. Instruct the children to fill their pockets with any number of each they wish. Compare the numbers of spoons to rulers.

21 Floor Rectangles

Using colored tape, make three 1 x 10 foot rectangles on the floor. Divide each rectangle into ten equal squares. Have the children sort themselves according to different characteristics. (Examples: Everyone with red shirts in rectangle A, blue shirts in rectangle B, and plaid shirts in rectangle C. Everyone with long pants in rectangle A, short pants in rectangle B, and dresses in rectangle C. Everyone who brought a lunch box in rectangle A, a paper bag in rectangle B, those eating cafeteria food in rectangle C.)

22 That's Me!

Copy each child's school picture onto the top of his/her sheet of paper. Have the child draw a picture of him/herself with long legs and long arms, or short legs and short arms, carrying something heavy or light, eating something big or little, etc. The children may choose to write captions for the pictures.

Fishing Pole
Attach magnets to the ends of fishing poles. Cut out ten different sea creatures. Attach paper clips. Let the children fish for a predetermined amount of time. Compare the "catches." Chart or graph the catches by laying them in straight lines next to one another.

Leaves
During the fall season, cut out and attach to the wall three or four paper tree trunks with bare branches. Collect three or four different kinds of leaves. Attach one variety of leaves to each of the trees. Count and compare leaves.

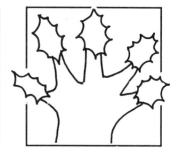

Shape Pattern
Put a three to four foot-long pattern of shapes on the floor or across a table for the children to copy. When they have successfully completed the activity, the children should put a three or four foot-long pattern of shapes on the floor for the teacher to copy.

Table Tennis Catch
Use markers to color numerous table tennis balls. Float them in water and give the children fish nets and a predetermined amount of time to gather the table tennis balls. Have the children sort them by color. Discuss who caught more or less of which color, how many of each were caught, etc.

Tunnel Crawl
On one side of a child's crawl-through tunnel, put a numeral pattern (such as 4, 9, 7, 6) on the floor. Have the children look at the pattern, crawl through the tunnel, and reproduce the pattern on the other side of the tunnel with the numerals provided. Shapes, color patterns, sizes, categories, etc., may be substituted.

28 Nuts

Provide a container of three to five different kinds of nuts. Encourage the children to pretend to be very neat squirrels who like to line up their nuts beside each other in rows containing only one kind of nut. Compare how many of each kind of nut are in each row.

29 Cowboy Hat Toss

One child tosses his/her hat into the air and attempts to catch it with his/her right hand. The class counts the catches; then the child switches to his/her left hand.

30 Monster Mouth

On a big box, put a picture of a monster who has a numeral in the middle of his stomach or head. This monster will accept only items in numbers that correspond to the numeral. The children can bring any items they wish to give the monster.

31 Bucket Catch

Roll colored foam rubber balls into a bucket or box. Compare and contrast the number of each color.

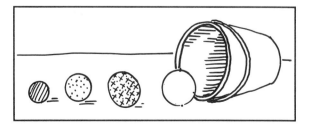

Numbers On My Back

Have the children close their eyes. Tape one numeral to each child's back. Have the children open their eyes, read each other's numerals, and then line up in numerical order.

Number Sit

Put numerals on chairs at one end of the room. Give each child standing at the opposite end of the room a picture of a number. On the "go" signal, each rushes to find the chair that matches his/her numeral and sits on it.

Clothespin Match

Divide the class into two groups. Use clothespins to put pictures of different number sets on the backs of children in one group. Clip the matching numerals on the backs of the children in the other half of the class. At the "go" signal, the children find their "number partners."

Music Math

Give pictures of number sets or numerals to each child. The teacher or another student sings the following song to the tune of "Are You Sleeping?"

If you have (8), if you have (8),
Stand up and shout.
Stand up and shout.

(The children who have "8" shout, "Eight!")

King/Queen Number

Make a crown on which there is a space to tape a numeral. Have large quantities of various items available. The king/queen will give out or accept items only in the quantity written on the crown.

37 Crazy Horse

Cut out the body of a horse without legs. Separately cut out numerous horse legs. Tell the children to make a silly horse with a number of legs that is different from the number of legs on a real horse. Compare the number of legs on each child's horse. Each child can write the numeral on his/her horse with a dark crayon and then color the horse all over with a lighter color.

38 Paper Plate Toss

Assign a number to each child. Draw or paint numbers onto paper plates. Mix the paper plates and let the children toss them into the air. On the "go" signal, everyone hurries to find the plate that matches his/her designated number.

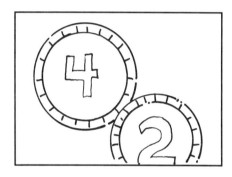

39 Giant Step

Count the number of giant steps, small steps, hops, broad jumps, skips, rolls, etc., that it takes to get from one point to another. Record the answers.

40 Egg Collection

Everyone pretends to be a rabbit. The mother rabbit tells the baby bunnies to gather colored eggs and tells them how many of each color to gather. Upon returning, each bunny tells how many eggs he/she gathered and how many of each color he/she gathered.

Number Me

Have each child make a number book about himself/ herself. Let him/ her draw or trace: one nose, two eyes, three toes, four fingers, five fingernails, six hairs, seven eyelashes, eight toenails. Each number should be on a separate page.

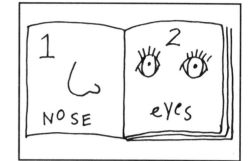

Toss It In

Give each child ten chances to toss beanbags into a bucket. Have the children note how many land inside and how many land outside the bucket. Have the children chart their responses by coloring one square red for each beanbag that landed inside the bucket and one square blue for each beanbag that landed outside the bucket.

Socks

Give the children a bag of old clean socks. Have them put as many socks on each hand as they can. Count and compare each child's socks.

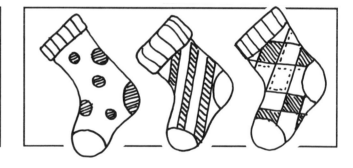

Cans

Fill the same-sized cans with various weights of materials, e.g., styrofoam pieces, sand, marbles, stones, nails, etc. Secure the tops with strong tape. Cover all the cans with the same pattern of self-adhesive paper. Seriate the cans by weight.

Tall Blocks

Provide 3" x 3" paper squares, some red and some blue. Allow the children to take as many of each color as they wish. They should tape them on the wall, one on top of another, building towers as high as they can while keeping their feet flat on the floor. Describe and discuss whose tower is taller/shorter, what combinations of colors were used, who used more/less of a certain color.

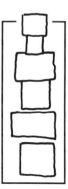

Leg Lift

One child sits on a table with his/her legs dangling. Hang a basket on one foot and have a second child put items (not too heavy!) into the basket for the first child to lift. Compare the weights of the items.

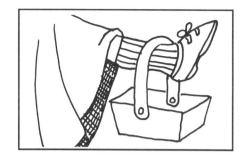

Kick The Carton

Each child decorates a plastic milk carton to make it easy to identify. The children stand in a line and kick the cartons as far as they can. Discuss which lands farthest from the line, which lands closest, whose carton is closest or farthest from his/her own carton, etc.

Box 'Em In

Have one large box and one small box available. See how many children can stand in each box, how many more/fewer are in each box, how many can sit in each box, etc.

Car Dice

Provide some large car dice, attached together with string. Have a child throw them and add the numbers that come up. He/she receives a corresponding number of squares, which are put into a line on the floor. After the children have had several turns throwing the dice, they may compare the number of squares in front of each child.

Measure
Allow the children to have free exploration with a variety of measuring cups, spoons, bowls, etc., in a variety of materials, e.g., sand, birdseed, water, flour, salt, etc.

Musical Innertubes
Put one innertube for each child on the floor. Play musical innertubes similar to musical chairs. When the music stops, each child gets into an innertube. Before you start the music again, remove one innertube. (Do this each time). If a child does not have an innertube, he/she joins another child inside his/her innertube.
Suggested questions: Which innertube has more/fewer children? Which has more/fewer girls? How many more children are in a particular innertube? Which has fewer jeans?

Melt
When it snows outside, allow each child to make a snowball and give each child an ice cube. Have them discuss which they think will melt first and estimate the length of time it will take each to melt.

Steps
Give each child a card with pictures of different items found in the classroom. Have the children count the steps they take from a designated line in the room to each pictured object. If appropriate, they can write the numerals.

Shout And Do
Give each child a numeral and sing the following song:
(Tune – "Old McDonald")
Teacher: (Mary Jane) has an 8.
Children: Yes, she has an 8.
Teacher: And (Mary Jane) can jump 8 times.
Children: She can jump 8 times.
Count/shout: 1, 2, 3, 4, 5, 6, 7, 8, while (Mary Jane) jumps 8 times.

Pitcher Pour

Have the children guess how many cups of water there are in a pitcher/container before pouring the water. Try the same activity with a differently-shaped pitcher/container that holds the same amount of water.

Flashlight

Tape pictures of sets/numerals around the room. Turn off the lights and shine a flashlight on one of the pictures. The children tell how many or what numeral they see. Each child is given the opportunity to shine the flashlight.

Shape Snowmen

Make paper snowmen with small, medium, and large triangles instead of circles. Substitutes: squares, diamonds, rectangles, ovals, etc.

Shape Poem

Tape or draw a large shape on the floor. (Several shapes may be drawn if it meets the needs of the class.) Act out the following poem:

    I'll jump in the (circle),
    Then what will I do?
    I'll jump out of the (circle)
    And I will pick you!

Number Sit

Give each child a numeral to secretly look at and then sit on. Have the children ask questions to find out what the hidden numeral is. Example: Is it more than _____ ? Is the number between _____ and _____ ? , etc.

Number Match Beads

Make pairs of numerals or numeral sets through ten. Shuffle the pairs and place them face down. Play number concentration to match the numerals or sets. When a match is made, the child gets that number of beads from a jar to put on a string. Compare the results.

Balloon Pop

Inflate up to twenty balloons. Use a marker to print numerals on each balloon. Allow the children to tape the balloons around the room while discussing number, size, and color. Have one child tell another child which balloon to pop. Example: "Pop the red balloon with the number 8 on it."

Animal Patterns

Put blocks in a line across the length of the classroom. Have the children put an animal on every other block. Discuss what is on the first, second, fifth, etc. block. Have the children "read" the patterns, "on, off, on, off", etc. Variations — put animals in front of and behind, under and on, etc.

Chair Steps

Line up five to ten chairs along a wall or scatter them around the room. Tape a numeral or picture of a numeral set on the back of the chair. The children read a number and step up on the chair that number of times.

Follow The Directions

A child is given a direction by child A, e.g., "Touch the door." Child B adds a second direction, e.g., "Sit at the teacher's desk." Child C adds a third direction, e.g., "Crawl under the table." The child has to follow the directions in the order given.

Stars

Number stars and place them on the wall. One child throws a beanbag, hits a numeral, identifies it, and performs an action (jumps, hops, turns around, etc.) that number of times. He/she picks another child who is then given a turn.

Purses

Fill a large purse with a large number of combs, lipsticks, and fingernail files. (Any three items found in a purse will do.) Give three other children smaller empty purses. One purse is for combs only, one for lipsticks only, and one for fingernail files only. Have the children pull an item from the larger purse and put it into the correct purse.

Clasp Hands

Whisper a number into each child's ear or secretly show the child a numeral. Have him/her draw that number of dots on the palm of his/her hand. Whisper another number into the same child's ear and have him/her write the numeral on the other hand. At the "go" signal, everyone must look at a friend's hands and match numeral to numeral set, clasping hands.

Tape It

Give each child a set of numbers or have the children cut out numerals. Have the children give each other directions, telling each other on which body part to tape the numerals. Example: Tape the 8 on your knee. Tape the 5 on your forehead.

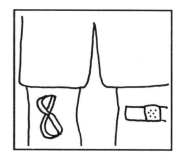

Paper Plate Toss

Have the children draw/glue a set of (4) items on the fronts of their paper plates and a set of (6) on the backs. On the count of 10, the children throw their plates up into the air. Have the children group together the plates that landed with the same number up.

    Variation: Instead of using two sets of numbers, you may use colors, big/little items, long/short items, etc.

Half A Plate

Provide one paper plate for each child. Give the child various numbers of stickers to stick onto the paper plate, with instructions to avoid placing stickers on the center of the plate. Have the child cut the plate in half and, on the count of 5, throw the two halves into the air. Each child then picks up any two halves, puts them together, and tells how many stickers he/she has and how many more/less he/she has than before.

Milk Carton Weight

Fill 15 half-pint milk cartons with sand. Tape them shut. Securely tape two cartons together. (Self-adhesive paper works well.) Tape three together, four together, and five together. You should have one left over, which gives you a set of one to five. Allow children to freely explore, line up by length, line up by weight, note which two equal another, etc.

Sidewalk Cracks

Encourage the children to count the number of sidewalk cracks he/she can jump over or how many times he/she can jump back and forth over one sidewalk crack.

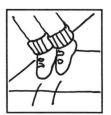

73 Tambourine Tune

Pull a numeral from a bag and play the tambourine or drum the corresponding number of times. Play the tambourine with different body parts—chin, thumb, finger, elbow, etc. Variation: Imitate a pattern played by another pupil.

74 Boots

Have each child fill one of his/her boots with whatever he/she wishes. Line up all the boots in an "empty, full, empty, full" pattern. Each child asks another for a boot that he/she would like to have, e.g., "the black boot that is empty." Children can count and discuss their "finds," e.g., "I have a brown boot full of blocks."

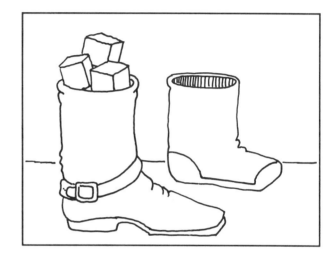

75 Hangers

Paste various categories of pictures, e.g., animals, food, clothing, etc., onto clip-type clothespins. Mix them together. The children clip similar groups together onto clothes hangers. Count, compare, and contrast categories.

76 Turkey Feathers

Give each child a turkey and let him/her paste any three colors of feathers onto the turkey's tail. Compare, count, contrast, etc.

77 Fence

Cut out and have available a variety of Halloween items that could be on a fence — 20 cats in three different colors, 20 pumpkins in three different colors, and 20 owls in three different colors. Provide or have the children draw a long fence. Encourage the children to glue cats, pumpkins, and owls in random order on the fence. Compare and contrast.

78 Circle Around

Provide large quantities of manipulatives, e.g., buttons, seashells, beads, cars, etc. Put other items, e.g., ruler, pencil, toy truck, on the floor. The children put the manipulatives around each item on the floor. Compare and contrast. The children may enjoy putting the manipulatives around themselves.

79 Flying Ghost

Let the children cut out small, medium, and large ghosts. They pick one and recite the following verse:

I'm the (smallest) ghost
And I can fly —
I can fly way up
In the sky.

80 What's In The Window?

Make five houses attached to one another accordion-style, small to large. Cut out windows which can open (one window in the first house, two in the second, etc.). The children can open the windows and put things inside.

81 Trees

Cut out five trees, attached accordion-style. Provide two different kinds of birds for the children to put into the trees. Compare and contrast the kinds of birds.

Flags

Give each child a blank flag and two or three different-colored stars to paste on as he/she sees fit. Compare and contrast the flags.

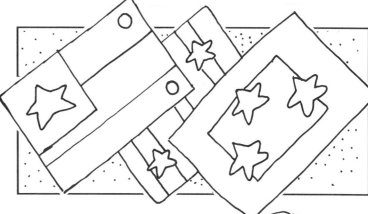

Rings

Provide two kinds of plastic Halloween rings, e.g., spiders and ghosts. Encourage the children to put on as many of each ring as they wish. Compare and contrast the children's choices.

Cotton Balls

Provide cotton balls in two colors and put them on a table. One child sits at each end of the table. Give each child a straw through which he/she blows to make the cotton balls roll off the table. Compare and contrast the cotton balls that are blown off the table. Compare and contrast how many of each remain on the table, how many more/less of each color are on the floor/table, etc.

Train Cars

Provide a large decorated oaktag train with four or five cars. Give four or five different manipulatives for the children to sort into different cars. Manipulative examples might include: animals, vegetables, clothes, furniture, and toys.

Shape Train

Have the children help you make a train with the cars made in different primary shapes (circle, square, triangle, oval, diamond, rectangle). Provide small cutout shapes or other manipulatives to be "put into" the train cars.

Sky / Ground

Divide a 12" x 18" sheet into sky (blue) and dirt (brown). Hinge a green sheet (grass) over the dirt. Provide objects that go in the sky, e.g., moon, rocket, star, kite, etc., and things that go in the ground, e.g., snake, worm, vegetables, rabbit, etc. Sort objects.

Christmas Tree

"Accordion" and laminate a group of three Christmas trees. Provide ornaments and candy canes for decorating. Have the children give each other directions. For example, one may say, "Put a candy cane on the third tree." Compare and contrast the numbers of ornaments and candy canes on each tree.

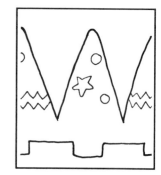

Spoons

Each child is given two spoons. Each child plays a pattern which the other children imitate.

Block Towers

Select building blocks in two colors and provide one of each color for each child. Have the children pick two items in the room they wish to compare and build a bar graph for each. Examples:

a. Stack up red blocks, one for each person who has long hair, and blue blocks, one for each person who has short hair.

b. Stack red blocks for those with pets, blue blocks for those without pets.

c. Stack red blocks for adults, blue blocks for children.

91 Pretzel

Explain to the children that a red bead will represent half a pretzel and a blue bead will represent a whole pretzel. The teacher or another student hides one of the beads in each hand and a child picks a hand. After seeing the color of the bead, he/she tells what he/she should be given—a whole pretzel or half a pretzel.

92 Vests

Provide construction paper shapes and tape. Let the children cut out paper bag vests. Each child chooses a partner to tell which shape *not* to tape onto his/her vest. Example: "Do not tape a circle. Tape whatever shape you pick on my left side."

93 Hats

Cut out and provide for the children a variety of hats in three different colors: twenty witch hats – black, brown, red; twenty hightop hats – black, brown, red; twenty derbies – black, brown, red. Encourage the children to draw as many stick figures as they wish on a long sheet of paper. They should then paste hats on the figures in any order they wish. Compare and contrast the hats.

94 Sand Spots

On paper plates, children write whichever numeral they wish with a marker. Then they trace it with glue and sprinkle it with sand. Around the numeral, draw a corresponding number of dots, lines, shapes, etc., trace with glue, and add sand. When everyone has finished, compare their products.

95 Get Dressed

Provide or have the children bring in different-colored pairs of mittens, boots, hats, and belts. (They will need at least three different colors.) Have one child give another child three instructions using ordinal numbers. Example: First put on the black belt, second put on the red hat, and last put on the yellow mittens.

96 It's In The Bag

Give each child three strawberry baskets and a bag filled with pictures of things in three categories such as animals, tools, foods. Examples: 5 animals, 3 tools, 1 food; 3 animals, 5 tools, 0 food; 2 animals, 1 tool, 4 foods. Each child pulls an item from his/her bag and puts it into the correct grouping in the strawberry baskets. (Three separate sheets of paper or three bowls may be used.) The children can compare the numbers of objects they obtained or compare objects with the other children.

97 Juice Containers

Fill and seal fruit juice containers with differently-weighted objects—sand, water, rock, styrofoam, rice, paper, etc. Roll each container down an incline or on a flat surface to determine which goes faster, farther, etc. Note the weight of the containers. Make a lever which the children can use to lift each container.

98 Baskets

Attach four pint-sized or quart-sized strawberry baskets together in a straight line or in a square. Attach a picture of a different category on each container. Provide objects which belong to the categories for sorting. You may choose to leave the category pictures off and allow the children to experiment with discovering categories on their own.

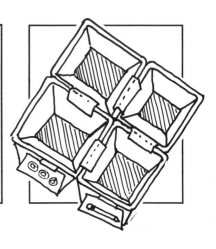

99   Fill 'Er Up

Use a string and tape to attach a small spoon, large spoon, plastic cup, bowl, cardboard container, and half-pint milk carton to separate quart-sized milk cartons. Provide sand, birdseed, styrofoam pieces, etc., for free exploration.

100   Take The Boat

Provide a child's swimming pool filled with water and some toy boats. On the floor next to the pool, put:
- different colors of one kind of object (such as bears, monkeys)   OR
- mammals and birds   OR
- people and animals.

The children take their boats across the water to bring back whatever they wish. Compare and contrast their loads.

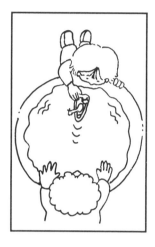

101   Colored Chalk

The teacher draws large shapes (circles, squares, etc.) on the sidewalk. The children are given colored chalk with which to trace or copy the shapes.

102   Pats And Kicks

Provide tape and numerous cutout hands and feet. The children may tape a hand on a friend's back or a foot on a friend's pants. Compare and contrast the numbers of hands and feet.

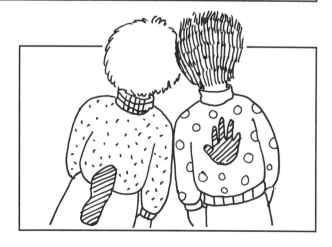

103 Pizza Toppings

Provide plain pizzas (decorated pizza boards) and two or three kinds of pizza "toppings," e.g., salami slices, mushrooms, olives, etc. Compare and contrast the amounts of pizza toppings.

104 Umbrella

Open an umbrella, turn it upside down, and hang it up a foot above the children's reach. Have the children throw balls in two or three different colors into the umbrella. Lower the umbrella. Line up the balls according to color and compare the results.

Example: ooo (red)
            ooooo (blue)
            oooooooooo (yellow)

105 Bus Load

Each of four or five children in a group receives a toy bus. At the other end of the room are animals, people, and various other toy objects. A number is selected, e. g., "5." Each child tells another what to bring back in his/her bus. Example: Bring back one dog, three cats, and one banana. The total number of objects brought back by each child must equal the preselected number.

106 Vegetable Paint Sticks

Tape or glue pictures of various vegetables on the ends of paint sticks and have the children "plant" them by standing them up in dirt, sand, styrofoam, etc. Discuss how many of each vegetable was planted, how many more/less than a friend planted, etc.

107 Suitcases

Provide small suitcases for the children to pack with pants, shirts, shoes, dresses, etc. Compare the numbers of items in each suitcase.

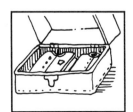

108 Sock Fill

Give each small group of children three different-sized socks – a baby's sock, a child's sock, and an adult's sock – to fill with a quantity of one item (e.g., all bears, all table tennis balls, all blocks, etc.). Compare quantities in each sock. Note weight, length, and size.

109 Paper Strips

Provide strips of paper in three different colors and three different lengths — short, middle-sized, and long. Encourage the children to take as many of each as they wish and to glue them onto a sheet of paper to make a picture. Discuss shapes found in the picture, how many of each color/length were used, etc.

110 Ribbon Hats

Provide narrow and wide strips of ribbon in two different colors. Provide paper plates which the children can decorate with the ribbons, making hats. Compare and contrast the hats, how many wide/narrow strips of ribbon were used, how many of each color, etc.

111 Bicycle Spokes

For each child, provide one small solid circle cut from construction paper and one large circle made from a long inch-wide strip of paper with ends taped together. The small circle should be placed in the center of the large circle. Provide different-colored strips of paper for bicycle spokes. Before the children begin taping the "spokes" in place, have them estimate how many they will need. Give the children a pattern of spokes to copy (e.g., blue, red, yellow, blue, red, yellow), or have them develop their own patterns. Compare the bicycle wheels.

Batter Up

Set up empty soft-drink cans as bowling pins. Give the children a bat, a medium-sized ball, and three crayons (each child should have the same colors). From a designated point on the floor, hit the ball with the bat and knock down as many pins as possible. Pick up all the pins that were knocked down and trace around the bottoms of them in a straight line on a sheet of paper. The children color the circles in colors of their choice. Count, compare, and contrast the drawings.

Pyramid

Put the numerals one to ten in the bottom of large juice cans. Tape the ten cans together in the shape of a triangle. Give the children items and have them put the correct numbers of items into each can.

Guess How Far

Draw a line on the floor. Tape different-colored lines five to ten inches apart and perpendicular to the drawn line. Provide a variety of objects — balloon, rock, beanbag, small pillow, ball, etc. The children guess which colored line an object will hit when it is thrown. Discuss how far each object went, which went farther and why, etc.

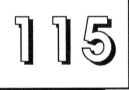

Copy, Please!

Pin various pictures to a clothesline, turning them away from the children. Each child picks a picture, examines it, returns it to the clothesline, and goes to the other side of the room to draw it. Examples of pictures:

a. Three trees with a monkey in two of the trees.
b. Four girls with only one of the girls eating an ice cream cone.
c. One woman with three baseball bats.

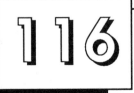

Band Leader

Put a different numeral on different musical instruments, e.g., a 6 on a drum, a 4 on a tambourine, etc. Each child picks an instrument. One of the children is designated band leader. He/she uses his/her baton to point to a child who plays his/her instrument as many notes as its numeral indicates.

117 Cats And Rats And Elephants

Make a deck of cards (approximately fifty) with pictures of cats, rats, and elephants, one animal per card. Set a timer for five to ten minutes. Put the children in small groups. The children take turns drawing cards and placing those that depict similar animals in a row. At the end of the time period, the rows are compared. (Any three animals or items may be substituted for the cats, rats, and elephants.)

118 Spin Around

Put a variety of objects having different weights, e.g., a feather, a sheet of paper, a toothbrush, a penny, a brick, etc., onto a lazy susan. Have the children spin it around quickly/slowly to determine what happens to each object.

119 Balls

Cut out numerous footballs, basketballs, and baseballs. Assign the numeral 2 to the footballs, the numeral 3 to the basketballs, and the numeral 4 to the baseballs. Put the numerals 1, 2, 3, and 4 on the four sides of a pyramid. The children in a small group take turns throwing the pyramid. Each child receives a ball of the type represented by the numeral that comes up when he/she throws the pyramid. For example, if a 3 comes up, the child receives a basketball. If the numeral 1 comes up, the child does not receive a ball. After all the balls have been claimed, the children compare the numbers of different balls that they have. (For this activity, any numerals will do. Assign numerals based on the needs of the children.)

120 Circle Actions

Have children seated in a circle on the floor. Each child silently thinks of a number from one to ten. One by one, each child performs an action a number of times that corresponds with the number in his/her head. For example, if a child thinks of the number 5, he/she could raise his/her arm five times, pat his/her head five times, stamp the floor five times, etc. The other children should imitate the action the same number of times and then shout, "Five!"

121 Hands Up!

Provide a huge sheet of paper, three or four different colors of water-soluble paint, and paintbrushes. Each child paints the palm of one hand and puts a handprint on the paper. He/she then paints his/her other palm another color and adds it to the paper. Have the children ask each other math-related questions.

Examples: How many more blue hands than red hands are there?
How many hands are there on the left side of the paper?
How many hands are there pointing to the ceiling?

As a variation, substitute feet for hands. It's more messy, but a lot more fun!

122 Rubber Band Can

Provide a large number of rubber bands in different colors and different sizes. Have the children completely cover a soft drink can or juice container with the rubber bands. Note any patterns, whether some rubber bands are too large or too small, which kind of rubber band takes up more space, which color is used the most or least, etc.

123 Dot-To-Dot

Use self-adhesive paper to make large numbers which you attach to the floor in a random or specific pattern. (A specific pattern might be a square, triangle, house, etc.). Anchor a string with tape to the number one. The children carry the string from number to number as they complete the number sequence. Anchor the string at each number. (A can filled with sand makes a good anchor.)

124 Pour And Fill

Provide five or six bottles or jars (preferably plastic and all the same size), various colors of tape, a fill material such as sand or rice, and a small scoop or spoon. Use the tape to mark each bottle to establish a fill line. Make sure these lines are at different levels. Instruct the children to fill the containers up to the tape lines. After all the containers are filled to the marked level, the children can arrange the contents by height. Later, remove the tape and have the children fill the bottles with varying amounts without the visual cues.

125 Animals In A Pen

Provide several pieces of string and some toy animals. Encourage the children to make shape "pens": circles, squares, triangles, etc. Model these if necessary. As children put their animals into the different pens, have them discuss how many are in each one, which pen has more/less of a particular animal, which pen is bigger/smaller, etc. If appropriate, numerals may be added to each pen, and the children can match the number of animals to the numerals.

126 Stuff It

Use small or medium-sized plastic juice bottles and cotton balls. Have the children stuff the cotton balls into the bottles until a predetermined time has elapsed. Have the children count the cotton balls they were able to stuff into their bottles.

127 Socks And Shoes

Provide a variety of socks that are of different lengths. Let the children put the socks in order from the shortest to the longest. Have available a supply of shoes in various sizes. The children should put these in descending or ascending order according to size and then match the shortest sock to the smallest shoe, etc.

128 Cheese And Crackers

Each child is given two to five crackers, a piece of cheese, and a plastic knife. Instruct the children to cut the cheese into pieces so that there is one piece of cheese for each cracker.

129 Lots Of Leaves

During the fall season, have the children collect a variety of leaves for sorting. They can sort them on the basis of kind, color, size, etc. They can also put the leaves in order from the smallest to the largest.

How Many Clothespins

Use slip-on type clothespins and cups/glasses of various circumferences. Place the clothespins on the rims of the glasses. Note which glasses need more/less/the same number of clothespins as other glasses (to go around the entire rim). As a variation, put the clothespins on different lengths of ribbon, paper, etc.

Chain Art

Provide different colors of construction paper and a pair of scissors for each child. Instruct the children to cut as many strips of paper as they want to make links to form chains. Encourage them to cut fat and skinny ones, short and long ones, different-colored ones, etc. When the children have cut out a number of strips, have them make their chains. Look for or encourage patterns. Measure to see whose chain is as long or as short as various objects in the room.

Clothespin Game

Cut out various shapes from construction paper. Put one to ten dots along the edges of each shape. (Laminate the shapes, if possible.) Encourage the children to attach a clothespin to each dot on each shape. The children can compare the shapes to determine which has the most/least clothespins attached. (Instead of plain dots, you might use pictures of animals, colors, numerals, clothing, etc. You might also choose to put these same pictures or corresponding pictures on the clothespins so that the children can match the pictures.)

Cups And Cup Rack

Provide five to ten plastic cups with handles, a cup rack or pegboard with cup hooks, and cubes of sugar. With a marker, put a number (depending on the needs of the pupils) on the bottom of each cup. The children may put the cups in numerical order while hanging them on the pegboard, or you may put numerals on the pegboard and the children can match the numerals. The children can also put the corresponding number of sugar cubes into the cups.

Box It Up

For this activity, the children will need five or six different-sized boxes and the same number of different-sized objects. The children should put the items in order by size and put the smallest item in the smallest box, the second smallest in the second smallest box, etc. Continue until all the sizes are matched.

135

Breakfast Cereals

Make up small bags/bowls of different kinds of cold breakfast cereals. Have the children sort the same kinds of cereal into piles. Talk about which bag/bowl has the most, least, same amount, etc. The children may count the pieces if they wish.

136

Which Has More?

Provide three clear jars which are all the same size. You will need items to count, e.g., cereal, buttons, blocks, small candies, etc. Place a different kind of item in each jar, being certain to vary the amount. For example, put five buttons in one jar, two blocks in another, and nothing in the third. Encourage the children to guess which jar has the most items in it and to tell how they came to their decision. The children may count out the items to determine which jar has more/less/the same. Children may be asked to determine why it takes more/less of a particular kind of item to fill up a container.

137

Same And Different

Give each child three or four objects, all the same except for one. Ask him/her to find the one that is different. Add and/or take away objects and ask him/her to find the two or three that are the same. The objects may differ in color, size, shape, function, classification, etc.

138

Shapes All Around

Cut pictures of objects depicting different shapes out of a workbook or magazine. Examples: a piece of pizza, a whole pizza, a record, a notebook, etc. Attach these pictures to index cards; laminate if possible. Divide a large piece of paper into four sections. Draw a different shape in each space. Encourage the children to sort the pictures by placing each one in the section with the appropriate shape.

139 Counting Box

Place a number of items in a large metal container or in a shoe box. Make sure that there is a different number of each item. For example, one button, two blocks, three miniature animals, etc., up to whatever number is appropriate for the children. Print the numerals on index cards. Let the children sort the items and match each set to the appropriate numeral.

140 Shapes And More Shapes

Cut a variety of shapes out of different kinds of wallpaper. Have the children sort the items by shape or by wallpaper design.

141 People Patterns

Have the children position themselves to form patterns. Examples:
Boy, girl, boy, girl, etc.
Tall, short, tall, short, etc.
Stand, sit, stand, sit, etc.
Front, back, front, back, etc.

142 Towers

Have a pile of blocks, cubes, etc., available for the children to use to build towers. After several minutes, signal the children to stop building. Make comparisons about the tallest/shortest towers. Count the blocks each child used to build his/her tower. Have the children determine how fewer blocks might make a taller tower, etc.

143 One To One

For this activity, you will need buttons or "wagon wheel macaroni." You will also need large cards. Divide the cards in half by drawing a line at the midpoint. On the top half of the card, glue a number of buttons or pieces of macaroni. The children should be encouraged to duplicate the quantity on the bottom half of the card. Have them count each set to see if the sets are the same, not enough, or too many.

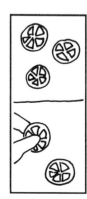

144 Pairs

Have each child put one of his/her shoes/mittens/socks into a pile in the center of the room. Mix up the items. At a signal, each child should find his/her shoe/mitten/sock to complete a pair. The children may determine how many of each color there are, how many have laces/buckles, how many more/fewer of each there are, etc.

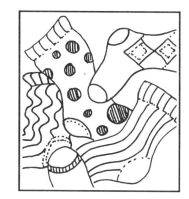

145 Puzzles

Cut large numerals out of construction paper. Laminate if possible. Cut the numerals into pieces corresponding to the numeral itself, i.e., #1–Uncut; #2–2 pieces; #3–3 pieces, etc.) The children put the pieces together to make the whole numerals and count the number of pieces in each numeral.

146 Count The Bugs

Make a beehive or spider web on a piece of paper (approximately 4" x 4"). Put a numeral on it. Laminate if possible. The children count out plastic or paper "bees/spiders" to match the numeral printed on the web/hive.

147 Number Necklace

Make number necklaces by printing one numeral on a small square/circle and attaching it to a piece of yarn. Each child picks a necklace to wear. The children put themselves in numerical order.

148 Houses And Furniture

Use boxes to make houses. Put a slit in the top of each box, and paint or draw a numeral on each house. The numerals chosen will depend on the needs of the children. Draw or glue varying quantities of furniture on small cards. The children match the number of furniture items on each card to the numeral on a house and put it into the slit.

149 The Bucket Game

Give each child a bucket or pail. Have each child select a number card from a stack of cards. Each child identifies his/her numeral, takes his/her bucket, and collects that number of items from around the room. After the items are collected, compare and contrast the items.

150 Toothpick Designs

Each child counts out three to ten toothpicks. Instruct each child to use the toothpicks to make a shape or design. After the initial designs have been made, have each child make a design with one more toothpick, two fewer toothpicks, etc. Compare the designs.

151 It's Growing

Select three or four vegetable or flower seeds to plant. Have the children plant each kind in a separate container. Label the containers. Observe the growth of the plants and record which kind grows first, second, third, last. The children can make predictions about which plant they think will grow first.

152 Fill It Up!

For this activity, you will need a variety of containers (different sizes, if possible) and a fill material (rice, beans, sand, water, etc.). You will also need scoops (spoons, ladles, cups, etc.). Make sure that each child's scoop is the same size as the others. Have the children predict how many scoops will be needed to fill their containers. As each child fills a container, he/she keeps track of how many scoops are used by recording each scoop on a chart. The child might color a square for each scoop, draw a line for each scoop, line up a car for each scoop, etc. Make comparisons among the different containers. Compare the actual number of scoops used to the predicted number.

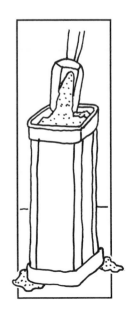

153 Keys And Chains

Give the children six keys and three key chains. Have him/her problem-solve to determine if the two sets are equal, how many more/less keys or chains are needed, etc. Repeat the activity by varying the original numbers of keys and key chains. You can also substitute toy horses and cowboys, bows and arrows, etc.

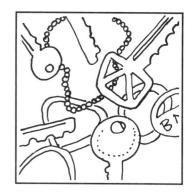

154 Barn Animals

Draw and cut out barns from red construction paper. Laminate if possible. Cut a door and fold it open. Tape pieces of white paper to the backs of the barns so they can be seen when the doors are opened. Print numerals on the white paper. The children open the barn doors, identify the numerals, and put a corresponding quantity of toy farm animals in front of each barn. You may choose to tape the barns to the bottom of a wall so they will stand up.

155 Pegboard Counting

Use a pegboard for this activity. Along the left-hand side of the board, run a strip of masking tape from the top of the board to the bottom. On the tape write numbers in line with the rows of holes until each row has a number. The children put pegs in the board to correspond to the number on the left, i.e., #3: place 3 pegs in that row.

156 Tie And Count

Cut a clothesline into various lengths. Make a series of knots in each length of rope. Blindfold or cover the child's eyes as he/she feels the knots to determine how many knots there are. Have the child count the knots with his/her eyes open to verify the number of knots. The child may also feel one rope while blindfolded and then feel two others to determine which has the same number of knots, which has more, or which has less.

157 Pancake Fun

Have the children help make pancake batter. Make three pancakes for each child, one small, one medium, and one large. Have the children arrange the pancakes on their plates from largest to smallest, or have them arrange them at random and discuss where the smallest pancake is, which of the pancakes is on the top, which pancake is on top of the largest pancake, etc. Add butter, syrup, and eat!

158 Daily Count

Place a number of objects, i.e., beads, pennies, marbles, etc., in a jar, box, or can. Change the number of items daily. Each day, a child counts the number of items and records the number on a chart or fills in a bar graph to show the number counted. Compare the amount to the previous day's amount.

159 High Card Low Card

For this activity, prepare at least forty 3" x 5" cards with one to nine dots or pictures on them. Have the children deal out all the cards and place them in stacks in front of themselves. They then take turns deciding whether the low card or the high card will win by saying, "High card" or "Low card." Each draws a card, and the winner receives both cards.

160 Chair Numbers

You can use this activity as part of a transition time. As you arrange chairs, carpet squares, etc., for a group activity, place a number card on each seat. As the children finish their previous activity, they take number cards from another deck of cards and then find their seats by matching their numbers to the ones on the chairs/carpet squares. Children can identify their numbers as the adult collects the cards.

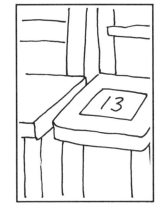

161 Daily Activities

Take pictures of the children involved in daily activities, i.e., hello time, playtime, worktime, snack time, gross motor time, good-bye time, etc. After these pictures have been developed, mount them on construction paper and make them available to the children so they can sequence the day's activities.

162 Snack Trays

Make number cards with the numerals from 1 to 5 written on them. Have available on a tray a large number of small snack items. The children select a numeral, identify it, and count out the same number of snack items. Each time the child wants more snacks, he/she has to select a numeral to tell how many can be taken.

163 Rock Shapes

Have available a supply of small rocks/pebbles. Encourage the children to use the rocks/pebbles to make various shapes. When all the children have finished making at least one shape each, have them count how many rocks were used. Compare the shapes each child made, i.e., bigger, smaller, the same size, which shapes used more/less/the same number, etc.

164 Set The Table

Place four place mats on a table. In a basket, place dishes, forks, spoons, knives, cups, and napkins. The number of each of these items should be greater or smaller than the number of place mats. The children "set" the table by giving each place setting one of each item in the basket. There will either be too many or not enough of the items. The children decide how many more of each item they need or how many extra of each item they have.

165 Cars

Draw or cut out roads of different lengths. Arrange these roads on the floor or table, making sure they begin at the same line. Using similar-sized matchbox-type cars, have the children place cars end-to-end on each road. Discuss which road has the most cars on it, how many cars there are on the longest/shortest road, how many more/fewer cars are on different roads, etc.

166 Coins

Provide nickels, dimes, quarters, pennies, and four different piggy banks. Attach a real coin or a picture of a different coin to each piggy bank. The children sort the coins by putting them into the properly designated banks.

167 Snowballs

During the winter months when snow is available, have the children make large and small snowballs. They may make four or five different-sized snowballs and then stack the snowballs in descending order. They may also line them up in random order and tell the ordinal position of their smallest/largest snowballs.

168 Fill In The Circle

Draw three circles on the floor. Number each circle depending on the needs of the pupils (1, 2, 3, or higher numbers for more advanced pupils). Give each child a different manipulative to count. The adult calls out, "One," "two," or "three," each child counts out one, two, or three objects and puts them into the correct circle.

169 Cooking

Suggest or let the children suggest a cooking activity, e.g., toast, eggs, gelatin, etc. Allow the children to decide what to do first, second, etc. Chart by drawings what the children decide should be done. Carry out the cooking activity in the correct sequence, and also chart this with drawings. Compare the two sequences. Discuss the differences and similarities in the drawings.

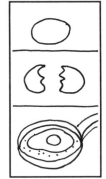

170 Felt Fun

For this activity you will need a felt board, a variety of small shapes made of felt, some numerals made of felt, and some pieces of paper or cards that can be drawn on. On each card draw a numeral and a corresponding number of shapes that are like the felt shapes (for example, draw two triangles on the card you have marked "2"). A child selects a card, "reads" it, and uses the felt pieces to duplicate the card on the felt board.

171 Rice Hunt

Bury miniature farm/zoo animals, 1 to 10 of each, in a large container of dry rice. Have the children dig for the animals and sort them into enclosures (aluminum pans, strawberry baskets, etc.) which represent the zoo or farm. Determine which enclosure has more/less/the same number of animals. Vary the categories—fruits, plastic numerals, colors, shapes, etc.

172 Apple Trees

Cut out various numbers of green, red, and yellow paper apples. Mix them together in a covered basket. Have each child pull out an apple and put it on his/her tree. At the end of a designated time period, compare the green, red, and yellow apples on each child's tree. (Be sure children are aware that in reality only apples of one color will grow on one tree.)

This activity may be varied by putting only one color of apple on three different trees.

173 Leopard Spots

Provide or have the children cut out a large leopard on which they can paste black and brown spots.

Compare the different numbers of spots that were placed on the various body parts.

174 Forehead

Cut out three shapes, at least ten of each, in three different colors. Example:

    circle—red, blue, green
    square—red, blue, green
    triangle—red, blue green

Have one pupil mix up the shapes and pass one shape out to each of the other pupils in random order. Each child attaches his/her shape to his/her forehead. The entire group decides if they will divide themselves into groups according to shape, color, both, etc. When a signal is given, they must divide themselves into these groups. If appropriate, a variety of sizes of shapes—large, medium, small—may also be introduced.

175 — Colored Squares

Use a marker to divide a square sheet of paper into 16 squares. Give each child a red, black, and green crayon, or any combination of three crayons. Put the crayons in a bag. Have the children each pick one crayon without looking and color any square. Continue coloring the squares until all have been colored. Note any patterns that develop, which color was used more/less, how many more/less than another, etc.

176 — Can Stilts

Fill pairs of cans with various weights of materials—rocks, styrofoam pieces, sand, birdseed, rice, etc. Tape a picture of the contents on the outside of the can. Secure lids on top of the cans and make them into stilts by attaching heavy strings for the children to hold. The children stand on the cans, hold onto the strings, and walk. Note which pairs are heavier/lighter, easier/harder to walk with, etc.

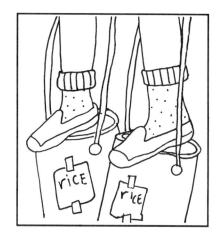

177 — Vases

Let the children make three flowers in three colors, using paper for the petals and stems, or pipe cleaners for the stems. Provide a vase for each child and encourage him/her to make a floral arrangement. Have the children determine how much of each color is used; which flowers are tallest, shortest, biggest, smallest, etc.

178 — Lotion Painting

Dip paintbrushes into small bowls of lotion. Paint shapes or numerals onto a blindfolded child's arm and have him/her identify what he/she feels.

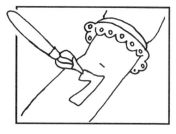

179 — Bowling Pins

Line up approximately ten bowling pins. Have each child throw a ball at the bowling pins. Note how many are knocked down and how many are left standing.

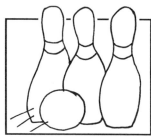

180 Frisbee®

Provide one Frisbee® for each child, each Frisbee® labeled with a different numeral. Take the children out to the playground and have all throw the Frisbees® at the same time. Each child should then locate a Frisbee® different from the one he/she brought outside. Each child reports which numbered Frisbee® he/she found and where it was found. Repeat activity.

181 Limbo

Have the children use sturdy blocks to build two equal towers as tall as the tallest child in the class. Put a rod or stick across the two towers and have the children limbo under the stick. Have the children remove one block from each side, and note how many blocks are left. Continue until the children can no longer limbo under the stick.

182 Monkey Food

Provide precut monkeys or have the children make their own. Attach the monkeys to a sheet of paper. Provide a large number of small bananas, peanuts, and apple wedges. The children pick the food for their monkeys and attach it to the paper. Discuss how many of each food item was used, which was used more/less/the same, etc. Instead of a paper activity, the children could provide food for stuffed monkeys using real or plastic food.

183 Paper Bags

Attach two sticks between two tables or chairs, and secure to them the open tops of three different-sized paper bags. Give the children the task of filling each bag until it breaks! Use blocks, canned goods, or any other items that might break the bags. It may be advisable to have a mat, some towels, or some newspapers under the bags. Let the children discover which bag holds more/less, how many more/fewer items are necessary to break each bag, etc.

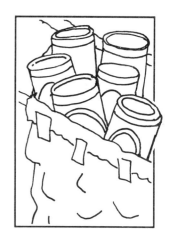

184 Kiss Or Gobble

Let each child choose a numeral to hold. The teacher holds a big puppet who is going to either kiss or gobble up numerals. The puppet asks, "Who has that delicious number (8)?" After a child answers that he/she does, the puppet asks, "Do you want me to give the number (8) a big kiss or gobble it up?" The puppet grabs the numeral and, depending on the child's wishes, either gives the numeral a big kiss or gobbles it up.

185 Balls Of Yarn

Have a child wrap the end of a ball of yarn around his/her index finger three times and then throw the ball of yarn. Another child cuts the yarn near the ball. The cut length is then compared to the length of the teacher's desk to see if it is longer, shorter, or the same length as the desk. The children can also compare the piece of yarn to the height of the door, the width of the window, etc.

186 Add On

One child tells the group how many times he/she wants them to perform an action, e.g., clap two times. The next child claps two times and adds another instruction, e.g., jump three times. Each child repeats the previous directions and adds another. Numerals may be repeated but can go no higher than a number decided by the class.

187 Can Can

Cut the tops off medium-sized cans, being very careful that no rough edges remain. Remove the labels if the children wish. Put numbers of small objects under each can. (The quantities will depend on the needs of the children.) Ask the children which quantity they would like to locate. Children take turns lifting a can to see if they have discovered the sought-after quantity. When a child finds the correct quantity, he/she takes possession of the objects and the game continues. At the end of the game when all quantities have been distributed, each child counts his/her total. Determine who has fewer, more, the same, how many more/less than another, etc.

188 Pipe Cleaner Bracelet

Provide a dish of round colored cereal with holes in it and a pipe cleaner for each child. Encourage the children to make a bracelet or necklace by stringing the cereal onto the pipe cleaner. Note and discuss patterns, quantities of each color, how many more/less of each color, etc.

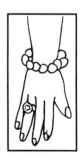

189 Mailbox

Choose four or five categories (such as cars, trains, buses, airplanes) and cut out ten pictures of items from each category (there will be 10 cars, 10 trains, etc.). Put each picture in an envelope. Have the children seal the envelopes, shuffle them, and put them in a mailbox. The children will take turns reaching inside the mailbox and taking out envelopes. Have them open the envelopes and sort the pictures inside. Then compare the numbers of items.

190 Craft Sticks

Have the children paint craft sticks in different colors. After the sticks dry, mix them up and have each child take five sets of four craft sticks. Each child makes a different design with each set of craft sticks and glues the designs onto a sheet of heavy paper or colored cardboard. Display the designs and note the variety of ways four things can look. Discuss which designs have more blue, which designs have no blue, which children have the same number of blue craft sticks, etc. Vary the numbers of craft sticks for different activities.

191 Space Satellite

Provide a styrofoam ball for each child and a large quantity of swizzle sticks or straws in different colors. Have the children make space satellites by sticking different colors of swizzle sticks into the styrofoam balls. Note the similarities and differences in the satellites, e.g., which has less red, which has no red, etc.

192 Numbers On The Floor

Tape numerals to the floor. Let the children give each other directions using the numbers. Example: "Run around the 5. Sit on the 6. Jump on the 7."

193 Pick Up A Ride

Provide a wagon and a selection of large numerals drawn on paper or other material. Give each child a numeral to hold, then ask the children to line up in random order. One child is chosen to walk by, pulling the wagon, shouting out one or two numbers. The child(ren) with the selected number(s) will then be given a ride in the wagon.

194 People And Cars

Give each child a toy car with built-in spaces for toy people, and a bag containing a number of toy people. Have the child place a "person" in each space. Talk about who has too many, not enough, etc., people for his/her car. Let the children determine if they need more and how many more they need. Have the children ask each other for the extra people.

195 Lines Of Toothpicks

Draw lines of different lengths with a marker on a long, flat piece of styrofoam. Place dots along the lines at $1/2$ inch intervals using different-colored markers. Give the children colored toothpicks and have them place a toothpick at each dot along the line. Compare and contrast how many toothpicks are used for the different line lengths. Look for color patterns.

196 Hammer Game

Place golf tees in a line on a large piece of styrofoam that is approximately 3 inches thick. Have the children use a small hammer to pound every other tee into the styrofoam. "Read" the design (in, out, in, out, etc.).

As a variation, have the children put small plastic bears, cats, or balls on every other tee. "Read" the design (on, off, on, off, etc.).

197 Bean Push

Cut small X's in the tops of margarine containers. Give each child a container and a supply of beans (a mixture of navy, lima, and kidney beans). Set a time limit and have each child push the beans through the X's into his/her margarine container. At the end of the determined time, have each child remove the top of his/her container. Make a graph showing how many of each bean were pushed through. Discuss more/less/the same, how many more/fewer, etc.

198

Caps

Have a supply of hats/caps for the children to put on as you sing this song to the tune of "Are You Sleeping?"

> Put two caps on,
> Put two caps on,
> On your head,
> On your head.
> Put two caps on,
> Put two caps on—
> On your head,
> On your head.

Change the number of hats or caps as you sing.

199

It's Far!

Using a ball of yarn or string, have the children help each other "measure" from their classroom to other points in the building, e.g., to the cafeteria, the library, the gym, etc. Cut the string after each measurement and have the children compare and contrast the lengths of the strings.

200

Boxes, Boxes, Boxes

Give each child a different-sized box with a lid. Have the children fill their boxes using items from around the room. When each child's box is full, have him/her put the lid on and return to the group. One by one, have the children count the numbers of items it took to fill their boxes and discuss which box has more or fewer items. Talk about why some children selected small or large items.

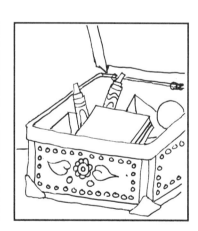

201

Find It

Hide different items around the room. (Seasonal items such as ghosts, pumpkins, witches, etc., are good.) Give each child a bag, and when the bell rings, everyone "hunts" for the specified items. When the bell rings again, everyone stops "hunting" and returns to the group. The children compare how many more/fewer/the same number of items they found.

202 We're Longer Than You

Have four children divide themselves into pairs. Each pair stretches out on the floor with one child's feet touching the other child's head. The remaining children decide which pair is longer/shorter and why. Continue with different combinations.

203 Feather Dusters

Give each child a bag containing feathers in different colors. The children are instructed to make as many feather dusters as they wish, but every feather duster must have feathers of only one color. Discuss how many feather dusters were made, how many feathers were used in each, which duster has more/fewer/the same, etc.

204 I'm All Arms

Have the children cut out a number of arms of different colors. Mix them all up, and then have them help each other tape arms on their backs, knees, shoulders, chests, foreheads, etc. Count, compare, and contrast the arms.

205 Magic Carpet Ride

Provide a piece of carpet that is long enough to hold several children. (An old sheet or blanket may be substituted.) Have a child pull another child on the carpet. Vary the number of children on the carpet and/or the number of children pulling the carpet. Discuss whether it was easy or difficult, how many children were pulling, and how many were riding.

206 Measles Madness

Cut out and distribute different numbers of red and yellow circles (bumps). Explain that on the right side of our bodies we are getting red bumps and on the left side we are getting yellow bumps. Tape the "measles" on the correct side. Count and compare the "bumps" on each side. Discuss which side has more/fewer; how many are on the stomach, elbow, etc.

207 Jelly Bean Jar

Fill the same clear plastic container with a different item each week (balls, blocks, styrofoam pieces, spoons, etc.). Once a week have the children estimate how many items are in the container. Keep a chart of the kinds of items and how many of each were in the container.

208 Stars And Moons

Cut out several stars and moons from foam rubber or carpet foam. Place them on a parachute or sheet. Have the children shake the parachute three times. Discuss how many items fly off, how many remain, etc. Number the items if appropriate, and discuss which numerals fly off, which fly farthest away, etc.

209 As Tall As I Am

Have the children use cans, blocks, milk cartons, etc., to build towers as tall as a selected item, e.g., the teacher's desk. Discuss how many of each item were needed, how many more/fewer of each were used, etc.

210 Feet On The Wall

One child lies on the floor and puts his/her feet against the wall. A second child draws a line on the floor at the top of the first child's head and writes the child's name. The children then change places so the other child can be measured. Have them talk about who is taller or shorter. Measure pieces of string from the wall to the drawn lines. Cut the strings and compare them.

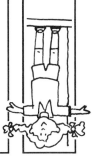

ACTIVITY SKILLS

Skill Content Areas ▼	Activity Numbers																													
	1	2	3	4	5	6	7	8	9	10	11	12	13	14	15	16	17	18	19	20	21	22	23	24	25	26	27	28	29	30
big / little		√																				√								
categories																														
charting					√																√		√					√		
combining & reducing sets																										√				
comparatives		√				√		√			√				√							√								
counting	√		√	√	√		√		√	√										√			√	√		√		√	√	√
distance																														
estimating																√	√													
measurement	√							√			√							√		√										
more / less same	√		√			√			√		√									√			√	√		√		√		
money identification																														
number recognition												√	√														√			√
ordinal position				√										√																
patterns										√																√	√			
right / left					√																								√	
set recognition												√	√																	
sequencing																														
shapes								√																	√					
sorting			√				√		√						√			√			√		√	√		√		√		

ACTIVITY SKILLS

Skill Content Areas ▼	Activity Numbers																													
	31	32	33	34	35	36	37	38	39	40	41	42	43	44	45	46	47	48	49	50	51	52	53	54	55	56	57	58	59	60
big / little																														
categories																														
charting												√							√											
combining & reducing sets										√																				
comparatives															√															
counting	√						√		√	√	√	√	√			√		√	√		√		√							√
distance																√														
estimating																						√			√					
measurement									√					√	√	√	√			√			√							
more / less same	√						√			√		√	√		√		√	√	√		√									√
money identification																														
number recognition		√	√	√	√	√	√	√																√		√			√	√
ordinal position		√																												
patterns																														
right / left																														
set recognition				√	√	√	√																	√	√		√			√
sequencing											√			√																
shapes																												√	√	
sorting										√											√									

57

ACTIVITY SKILLS

Skill Content Areas ▼	Activity Numbers																														
	61	62	63	64	65	66	67	68	69	70	71	72	73	74	75	76	77	78	79	80	81	82	83	84	85	86	87	88	89	90
big / little	√								√										√											
categories														√																
charting									√																					√
combining & reducing sets										√																				
comparatives									√		√																			
counting	√								√	√		√			√	√	√	√		√	√	√	√	√	√			√		√
distance																														
estimating																														
measurement											√																			
more / less same										√					√	√	√	√		√	√	√	√	√				√		√
money identification																														
number recognition	√		√		√		√	√					√							√										
ordinal position																														
patterns		√												√															√	
right / left																														
set recognition			√		√		√	√		√			√							√	√									
sequencing				√																										
shapes																											√			
sorting						√			√							√					√				√	√	√			

58

ACTIVITY SKILLS

Skill Content Areas ▼	Activity Numbers																													
	91	92	93	94	95	96	97	98	99	100	101	102	103	104	105	106	107	108	109	110	111	112	113	114	115	116	117	118	119	120
big / little																														
categories								√																						
charting														√								√								
combining & reducing sets				√																						√				
comparatives	√																		√	√								√		
counting			√			√				√		√	√	√	√	√	√	√	√	√	√	√	√		√	√	√		√	√
distance																								√						
estimating																								√						
measurement									√									√						√						
more / less same			√			√	√			√		√	√	√	√	√	√	√	√	√	√	√	√			√		√		
money identification																														
number recognition				√																	√		√			√			√	√
ordinal position					√																									
patterns																					√									
right / left		√																												
set recognition															√									√	√	√				√
sequencing																														
shapes											√																			
sorting	√					√		√				√					√										√		√	

59

ACTIVITY SKILLS

Skill Content Areas ▼	Activity Numbers																													
	121	122	123	124	125	126	127	128	129	130	131	132	133	134	135	136	137	138	139	140	141	142	143	144	145	146	147	148	149	150
big / little					√		√		√					√								√								
categories																														
charting																														
combining & reducing sets		√																												
comparatives							√				√											√								
counting	√	√	√		√	√		√		√	√	√	√		√	√		√		√		√	√	√	√	√		√	√	√
distance																														
estimating																√														
measurement				√							√											√								
more / less same	√	√		√	√					√				√	√						√	√	√						√	√
money identification																														
number recognition			√		√								√						√						√	√	√	√	√	
ordinal position																														
patterns											√										√									
right / left	√																													
set recognition					√								√			√			√				√					√	√	
sequencing			√	√			√		√					√													√			
shapes					√							√						√		√										√
sorting	√						√		√		√				√	√	√	√		√				√						

60

Skill Content Areas ▼	Activity Numbers																													
	151	152	153	154	155	156	157	158	159	160	161	162	163	164	165	166	167	168	169	170	171	172	173	174	175	176	177	178	179	180
big / little		√					√						√				√							√			√			
categories																					√									
charting		√						√											√											
combining & reducing sets																														
comparatives	√																									√	√			
counting		√	√	√	√	√		√				√	√	√	√		√	√		√	√	√	√		√		√		√	
distance																														
estimating	√	√																												
measurement		√																												
more / less same	√																			√	√	√		√		√		√		
money identification																√														
number recognition																		√		√								√		√
ordinal position				√	√					√		√					√		√											
patterns																									√					
right / left																														
set recognition				√	√				√						√			√		√										
sequencing							√				√							√	√											
shapes													√												√					
sorting																				√	√	√	√			√				

ACTIVITY SKILLS

Skill Content Areas ▼	181	182	183	184	185	186	187	188	189	190	191	192	193	194	195	196	197	198	199	200	201	202	203	204	205	206	207	208	209	210
big / little			√																	√										
categories									√																					
charting																	√										√			
combining & reducing sets																									√					
comparatives	√		√		√						√				√				√			√		√						√
counting	√	√	√		√	√	√	√	√	√	√			√	√		√	√		√	√		√	√	√	√	√		√	
distance																	√											√	√	
estimating																											√			
measurement	√				√														√			√							√	√
more / less same	√	√	√				√	√	√	√	√			√	√		√		√	√			√	√	√	√		√	√	
money identification																														
number recognition				√								√	√															√		
ordinal position																														
patterns								√							√	√														
right / left																										√				
set recognition								√																						
sequencing																														
shapes																														
sorting								√	√		√												√			√				